Anne Duval

# HOUSEPLANTS

## for Beginners

**A Complete Guide to Choose, Grow and Take Care of your Houseplants**

# Table of Contents

# Introduction

At one time or another most everyone had a plant or two in their house or apartment. If you have a bit of a green thumb, your plants grew and offered you hours of enjoyment or maybe you even had a name for each plant. Yes, you are indeed the talented ones who can grow just about anything anywhere.

Then there is the beginner house plant owner who with the best of intentions looked on in dismay as they watched their plants slowly wither away eventually becoming nothing more than a dried stick. You ask around for help and one of your friends may say, "You probably didn't give it enough water." Yet another friend would say, "The problem is giving your plant too much water."If as a plant owner this sounds familiar then you're not alone, you just need a little bit of advice on what to do for your plants as well as what not to do.

Houseplants for Beginners is a guide to house planters and a starting place for those of you who don't know much about plants but want something green in their homes. This book is designed to help you "bone up" on some of the more commonly found plants and to give you the basic knowledge of what the plants need in order for you to be a successful grower.

You'll find the profiles of different houseplants—from the common aloe vera plant to the exotic chocolate conidium orchid—that boast impressive health-giving qualities. Some of them purify indoor air of harmful toxins. Others are great for making tonics, poultices, and tinctures that can be used to treat all manner of conditions, from stomach upset to skin irritation to blocked sinuses.

This book will help you as a beginner house plant owner and I hope you will find tips and suggestions that will help you grow healthy, strong, and vibrant plants that will be admired by any visitor to your home.

I suggest you start with growing one or perhaps two plants, and when you learn how to nourish them to become strong and healthy, you might want to grow a variety of other plants. Yes, even vegetables such as tomatoes, lettuce, spinach, Swiss chard, and most herbs.

Now it's time to move forward.

# The Benefits of Houseplants:

Houseplants don't only liven up your home or give you a touch of nature to enjoy, they are also very beneficial to humans.

**Some of these benefits are:**

- Plants and humans have opposite breathing patterns to humans to give us fresh oxygen during the day. They filter the carbon dioxide in the air and release oxygen.

- Plants can act as natural humidifiers as they release around 97% of the moisture they take in during the day.

- Plants also remove toxins from the air such as harmful chemicals like solvents, cigarette smoke and so on. These harmful toxins are referred to as Volatile Organic Compounds (VOC's). In a building that is airtight and or has air conditioning, plants are the key to purifying the air.

- Studies have shown that plants can improve personal health, they are soothing and tend to liven up a room. In hospitals, there has been some research done by the Kansas State University that showed the patients that had plants in their rooms recovered a lot quicker.

- They make work environments seem less sterile and have proven to increase productivity.

- In colleges, there have been numerous studies that showed a classroom with plants improved students' concentration.

- It is common knowledge that a green room can relieve stress, reduce blood pressure and help to improve a person's mood.

# Choosing Your Plant(s)

Initially, it is almost like going to get a dog for the first time. You have to decide are you going to get a baby one, teenager or full-grown! Then there is the chicken or the egg scenario; what comes first finding the right spot for the plant(s) or finding the right plant for the house/office?

See it is kind of like choosing a pet for the first time! The trick is not to over think it rather take a walk around your space and try to visualize where you would place a plant. Or if you have a plant in mind, where do you think the best spot for it would be.

**For either your home or office, ask yourself:**

- What space(s) do you want to fill in your home/office?
- Do you need the plant to rest on the floor or a table/shelf?
- Does the position receive a lot of light?
- Are you looking for a flowering plant or not?
- How much maintenance are you willing to do or have time to do?
- Most importantly, how much are you wanting to spend on buying the plant (keep in mind there are other costs involved in houseplants).
- Do you have colors in mind?
- Do you have a theme in mind?

## Go window shopping for plants

Yes, it is a thing! You can "window shop" for plants. Plant nurseries and garden centers these days are awesome. They have so much more than just plants in. In fact, you could probably spend an entire day in some of the larger ones.

A lot of the new plant nurseries or garden stores have lovely coffee shops. These are specifically designed to give you a great plant experience. You sit amongst the plants, running waterfalls and ambiance of the surrounds taking it all in. Even the busiest of nurseries have a sort of tranquility about them. The bustle just seems to become white noise when surrounded by plants, garden accessories and of course the sound of fountains.

These centers are filled with plants and usually, have qualified staff who can help advise you on the best plant(s) for your space(s). Once you have a good selection to choose from you will know how many you will need, and the garden center will also be able to best advise you on the plants care or any special instructions.

## Research

This is where this guide comes in. The best way to figure things out is with a bit of research. There is so much out there these days on the internet, the shelves in stores are filled with gardening books of all kinds.

In fact, there is way too much information out there, so much so that you will go into information overload. All that does is cause even more confusion and make a person want to scream or just go buy plastic plants!

But before you rush off and think that plastic is the best option as you cannot kill it, stop and finish reading through this guide to see that you do not need to be a botanist or have the proverbial green thumb. Just some good, easy to follow advice, tips, and tricks to get you on your way to bringing a bit of nature into your home.

I will guide you through some easy steps to get started, how to choose that correct spot for your plant, which plants are best for beginners along with a lot of other helpful tips without the information overload.

# Best Houseplants for Beginners

Renting plants may be a good option to test the waters but we cannot all afford that. Plus, they do not always have the plants we want, and you are at their mercy. Choosing your own is part of the exciting new adventure into bringing nature indoors for your benefit, enjoyment and to make your house a home.

## The Peace Lily

If you are looking for a plant that flowers, is low maintenance but at the same time elegant and adaptable this is the plant. The Peace Lily has beautiful dark green leaves and stems with an elegant white flower that is yellow at its center. They do not require much room and the plant will grow upward with a hardy stem that does not droop. It grows and conforms to the shape of its pot. Not only are they one of the easiest plants to grow indoors they will change the dynamic of any spot you put them. They are better suited for a shelf or countertop type environment.

## Bromeliads

If you are looking to bring some warm color into an area and you do not have much room, then Bromeliads are best. They thrive indoors and will stay to the confines of their potted environment. These plants also come in an array of beautiful warm colors, although to be honest they are easy to grow but are really stubborn when it comes to flowering. If you want them for their flower, try to buy plants that are already in bloom. Their flowers last a long time, but they do not always bloom and can take forever to do so. Even if they do not flower their leaves have beautiful color arrays on them and those in flower usually have a few different colors to display.

## Snake Plant

This is one of the most popular houseplants and is also the best for beginners. They are not that easy to kill and require minimal watering. These plants need so little, but they give so much. They will remove all the toxins from the air, provide sufficient humidity to the room and do not require excessive lighting. They are the perfect houseplant for anyone. The one thing that you can do though is over water this plant which will cause the soil to rot. Their leaves are shaped like daggers and are a sturdy green with white/off-white patterns around the edges and lightly striped across them. They are great for off and on the shelf as they grow to the size of their pot or environment.

## The English Ivy

This is a very pretty plant that adapts to its potted environment although it does creep being a creeper type plant. You will have to watch it and keep it pruned or it will try to take over its surroundings. That being said, it is still a very easy plant to grow and maintain. They do not like direct sunlight and prefer their pots to be shallower and long rather than tall and deep. They are not flower bearing plants but have pretty little green leaves that are edged with an off-white to light pinkish leaves that are shaped like a small elephant's head or long heart shape. Once again this is a very hardy plant that does not quite very easily, so it takes a lot to kill it.

## Cacti

If ever there was a plant for beginners, it is a Cactus. In fact, some of them do not need to be in soil to grow. They come in all shapes and sizes and are extremely great for Feng Shui gardens in a house or tiny miniature gardens in a long planter. There are round ones, tall ones, spikey ones and they all usually get flowers or have some form of a flower on them. They will go without water for ages, most do not need direct sunlight or a lot of attention at all. There is a reason these plants can survive desert conditions, but care must be taken with the thorns as there are those that have a bite to them. Sometimes the bite can be pretty severe so always check on the plant's toxicity levels.

## Peperomia

Although they do like their water or mist spray, they are very hardy plants. They also have beautiful swirling leaves that come in different shapes, sizes, and colors. These leafy plants bring shape and splash of magnificent green to any space they are in. They prefer to be on a shelf or tabletop environment. Another excellent plant for beginners requiring minimal maintenance and not too much space. Plus, they have a rather relaxing look about them.

## Dracaena

These plants look like long arms with spiky green poms at the top of them. Their stems look like a rope that is twined with white and green. The leaves are long and green sometimes they have some warm shades of orange and red on them. They are the perfect plant for that floor corner or just off to the side of a window. They do not like a lot, if any, direct sunlight and require occasional watering as well as pruning. These plants are really easy to grow as well as take care of and they are so elegant to look at they bring any floor space to life.

## The ZZ Plant

This is the houseplant to get for those that want to make a start with houseplants but have had their fair share of disasters. It is very strong, hardy plant that requires little maintenance is great to look at and will grow within the confines of its potted environment. Plus, it may not happen often, if ever, but it gets an unusual flower on it. It is a spathe-type flower that makes it look like it is shyly peeping out at the world through curtains. The flower almost looks like that of the Peace Lilies, but it does not open up as wide and the petals stay a green color.

## When in Doubt, Ask!

There is no shame in asking what, where and how when it comes to plants. These are directions that you need to be aware of to ensure you can take proper care of your plants.

You may think all they need is a bit of water, maybe some fertilizer here and there or some pruning! But, like any living thing, plants have special instructions attached to them. Some need more sunlight than others; some need less water than others or regular soil changes whilst some are basically self-sufficient and like cats only really need you when they need you!

If you have children or animals in your home, it is always best to find out about the toxicity of the plant. Quite a few plants can cause serious harm to humans and animals, so it is best to seek advice before taking the plant home and having an incident. Even if you do not have kids or animals on your own you should find out. You never know what might happen and having all the details on hand could very well save a life or prevent serious illness.

# The Basics of Houseplant Care

Plants in good health actually use carbon dioxide in the air and produce oxygen, making tropical plants with big leaves particularly popular with those who want to improve the air quality of their homes. To get this benefit, however, the plant needs to be healthy and growing. Following are some general tips on plant care.

## Soil

Potting soil is generally used for tropical houseplants. A good potting soil is a peat moss with some perlite mixed in. The perlite will be small white particles in the peat moss. Since the perlite is there to aerate the soil, you may want to add more to the mix than has been provided. Perlite can be purchased separately in small bags. Adding a scoop or two to a bag of potting soil will help the potting soil from becoming packed. Even though a plant's roots are covered in soil, they do receive some air. Packed soil eventually suffocates the roots and damages the plant. Plants that like drier soil, such as succulents, should be potted in a potting mix. This is not the same as the peat moss potting soil. A potting mix is drier, holds less water and allows more air to the roots. Some potting mixes can be improved by adding perlite to the mixture, if the mix seems too heavy, or with a scoop or two of the potting soil, if it seems too dry and crumbly.

## Containers

Most people want a container that is attractive but doesn't leak water. Many containers come with built in saucers that may or may not be sufficient to catch the run off when the plant is watered. If this is a concern, you may want to use a cache pot, which is a pot with no hole in the bottom. These usually hide ugly plastic pots and catch the run off with no danger of water spilling onto furniture or floor. Cache pots can be purchased, or other types of old crocks or containers that will hold water can be put to use as a cache pot. Regardless of whether you use a pot and saucer or a cache pot, when you decide to re-pot your new plant, the new container should only be slightly bigger than the old container. For example, a plant in a 4" pot should be potted into a container that is no bigger than 6". Moving up a size is typically referred to as potting up.

## Feeding

A couple of ways to feed houseplants are to either use the slow release pellet type of fertilizer or the water soluble fertilizer. The pellets are mixed into the soil when the plant is re-potted and the nutrients are absorbed over time. The pellets last around 6 months, so if you keep your plant in the same container longer than that, you may need to start top feeding. The water-soluble fertilizer is mixed with water and, if mixed as a weak solution, can be used for each watering, giving the plant a little food each time. Although sometimes a pain to mix or store, it is easy enough to do. Each fertilizer will have three numbers on the label that tell the ratio of nitrogen, phosphate and potash in the mix. A fertilizer that has all numbers the same or the middle number slightly higher is fine for houseplants.

## Watering

Most houseplants can do well with once a week watering. That doesn't mean, however, that they all need the same amount of water each week. Some prefer moisture while others would rather stay somewhat dry. For those that like moist soil, it is better to give the plant a little water twice a week than a lot of water once a week. Few plants like to sit with their bottoms in water, mainly because water-logged soil suffocates the roots. Some have a need for humidity. Plants that prefer humidity may thrive in a bright bathroom where showering increases the humidity level each day. Another option for smaller humid-loving plants is to plant them in an enclosed terrarium where the moisture can be contained.

## Light

Available light is one of the most important elements to growing houseplants successfully. Your home or office receives morning and afternoon sun on the east and west sides of the building each day (unless shaded by trees or other structures). In North America, the north facing wall of your house or office receives sun all day in the summer and is shaded in the winter. The south facing wall receives sun all day in the winter and is shaded in the summer. The intensity of the sun shining through any of these windows depends on how far south you are. Some plants can take direct sun through an un-shaded window, others cannot. For those that cannot take full direct sun, the light has to be filtered by the external shade of a tree or covered porch or by sheer curtains or partially open blinds. Some plants cannot take filtered light for very long and prefer "indirect" light. Indirect light is bright light without any sun shining through the window onto the plant, the equivalent of a west window with the blinds mostly closed.

## Pests

Although this book does not contain information about controlling pests, the typical use of insecticide is either through spraying the leaves of the plant, using a dust on the leaves or by using a granular systemic insecticide. The systemic is mixed into the soil and is taken up by the plant through the roots, making the entire plant an insect no-go zone. Since the systemic is designed to be absorbed, it can also go through the skin and should only be handled with gloves. Although a great way to protect the whole plant over time, this may not be something you want to do if you have young children who may want to dig in your "dirt" or pets who may want to do likewise.  The use of sprays or dusts may also pose a real risk to pets that may chew on plants.  Although some plants are toxic by nature, using insecticides will make all parts of the plant toxic, including the potting soil.

\

# Lighting for Your Plants

Plants do not only count on water and fertilizer to grow but also light. Some plants love to bask in the full rays of the sun while others prefer the light but not direct rays and then some prefer to be in the shade with a bit of humidity. Now, we are going to look at understanding natural light and how to simulate light if your house or apartment does not get a good amount of natural light.

## Why a Plant Needs Light

Photosynthesis is a process whereby plants use the nutrients they trap from the watered soil which is mixed with the carbon dioxide they absorb from the air to produce their food. The plant gets the energy to power this process from the sun which is trapped by the chlorophyll in the leaves. The chlorophyll is the green pigment in the leaves and in turn helps the plant give off clean oxygen for us to breathe.

## The Flow of Natural Light in a House or Apartment

One of the biggest challenges for an indoor gardener is finding the correct lighting conditions for their potted plants. You may think that a sunny window creates enough light, but it is important to note that the sunlight may stream in through large glass windows, but that light is not nearly as intense as it is in the great outdoors.

That is why it is very important to consider which way a window is facing to gauge the intensity of the sun through the windows during the day. The following guide is based on windows mainly for North American houses and or apartments.

## Windows that Face South

Windows that face south usually get the most intense light throughout the day. For plants that like a lot of direct sunlight this is the window or as near to it as possible that you should place them.

For plants that like the light but not direct light you may want to position the plant a little away from the window.

## Windows that Face East

These windows are good for plants that like moderate or morning sunlight as they tend to get the most sunlight during the morning and will move to shadow in the afternoon.

The rays are also not as strong in the morning so if the plant is in the direct light, it will not feel as intense as the rays of a southern facing window. They will not be left in the sun for very long either as it moves through to the afternoon position.

## Windows that Face North

North facing windows are more for a plant that likes to live in the shade and usually only get warm during the summer months. In winter North facing windows are not very good for growing plants.

It is best not to use these windows for growing plants and rather put plants that love the shade in the more protected areas of the room that are adorned with east or west facing windows.

## Windows that Face West

West facing windows get the full force of the midday and afternoon sun. In the summer months, this can be rather strong and is a good place to position plants that love to soak up the full force of the sun's rays. In the summer months, these windows tend to keep warm into the early evenings.

This is not a good place to put plants that only like indirect sunlight as they could get damaged from overexposure to the sun. But finding a great shady spot in the rooms that feature these windows is a good position for plants that like indirect light and warm brightly lit spots.

## How to Measure the Intensity of Light in a Room

There are various meters a person can buy on the market today that will measure the intensity of light in a particular room at various times of the day.

The old-fashioned way is to do so by measuring the shadow it casts in the room. A strong sharp intense beam means it has a high/bright light, and shadow that is a bit less defined is of moderate intensity and a room that gets no light shadow is of a low light.

## Creating Light for Houseplants

Getting the best lighting for indoor plants is quite a challenge as you have to find the correct space in the house where the sun flow is just right. With seasonal changes, it means having to reposition the plant as the sun in the wintertime is nowhere near as strong as in the summer.

Then there is the lack of space a person may have in a house or apartment or not enough windows to accommodate the plants. One way to help houseplants get enough light is with artificial lighting.

It is important to remember when using artificial lighting that the plants will need at least twelve hours a day of darkness. Just like we do, plants go through day and night processes so if you are emulating daylight you will need to give them a period of the night as well. Most lighting options that are specifically designed for growing plants do come with sophisticated timers that will automatically switch them off during the night.

There are a few options a person can look at to help increase the light flow for houseplants:

## For Larger Spaces - Halide Lighting

Halides are not cheap and are more for the serious plant atriums or larger room spaces. These tend to be large bulbs that are used for growing vegetables or larger plants and are found in hothouse environments. They are sophisticated lamps that can be set to provide plants with a good eighteen hours of intense light.

This type of lighting is better for plants that need intense direct sunlight to thrive.

## Fluorescent Lighting

These are the most commonly used and are for indoor plants that need a moderately warm, bright and lower lighting requirement. They can be set to make a nice warm sunny environment for plants and come in varying ranges of T5, T8, and T12. They are not as expensive to run as the Halides are.

With fluorescents, they are a long tubular bulb and the thinner the bulb the brighter it is, the thinner ones tend to be more efficient as well.

## Incandescent Lighting

Incandescent lights tend to light up a room nicely, but they are not very energy efficient for plants as only around ten percent of their light can be used for energy whilst the rest of the light gives off heat. These lights are good for plants that have a medium to low-lighting requirement.

## Plants Best Suited for:

### INDIRECT LOW LIGHT

- ❖ Bamboo Palm (also known as reed palm)

Bamboo Palm-Prefers frequent watering, keep soil moist.

- ❖ Birds Nest Fern

Birds-nest-fern- Prefers frequent watering, keep soil moist.

- ❖ Chinese Water Evergreen

Chinese water evergreen- Prefers frequent watering, keep soil moist.

- ❖ Cast Iron Plant

Cast Iron Plant-Prefers frequent watering, keep soil moist.

- ❖ Corn Plant (can be grown in indirect bright light).

Corn plant- Prefers infrequent watering, soil surface dry to touch before watering.

- ❖ Grape Ivy

Grape Ivy- Prefers infrequent watering, soil surface dry to touch before watering.

- ❖ Holly Fern

Holly fern- Prefers frequent watering, keep soil moist.

❖ Heart Leaf Philodendron

Heart leaf philodendron- Prefers infrequent watering, soil surface dry to touch before watering.

❖ Lady Palm (can be grown in indirect bright light)

Lady palm- Prefers frequent watering, keep soil moist.

❖ Maidenhair Fern (can be grown in indirect bright light)

Maidenhair fern- Prefers frequent watering, keep soil moist.

❖ Parlor Palm

Parlor Palm- Prefers frequent watering, keep soil moist.

❖ Pothos Plant

Pothos plant-Prefers infrequent watering, soil surface dry to touch before watering.

❖ Peace Lily

Peace lily-Prefers infrequent watering, soil surface dry to touch before watering.

❖ Swedish Ivy

Swedish- ivy- Prefers frequent watering, keep soil moist.

❖ Wax Plant (can be grown in indirect bright light)

Wax plant- Prefers infrequent watering, soil surface dry to touch before watering.

# INDIRECT BRIGHT LIGHT

- ❖ African Violet

African violet- Prefers frequent watering, keep soil moist.

- ❖ Asparagus Fern

Asparagus fern- Prefers frequent watering, keep soil moist.

- ❖ Avocado

Avocado- Prefers frequent watering, keep soil moist.

- ❖ Cordyline

Cordyline- Prefers infrequent watering, soil surface dry to touch before watering.

- ❖ Ficus (Many varieties belong to the fig genus)

Ficus- Prefers infrequent watering, soil surface dry to touch before watering. Needs lots of humidity best to use humidifier.

- ❖ Jade Plant

Jade plant- Prefers infrequent watering, soil surface dry to touch before watering.

- ❖ Snake Plant (Sometimes called Mother-in Law's Tongue)

Snake plant- Prefers infrequent watering, soil surface dry to touch before watering.

- ❖ Spider Plant

Spider plant- Prefers frequent watering, keep soil moist.

- ❖ Warneck Dracaena (can be grown in indirect low light)

Warneck dracaena- Prefers infrequent watering, soil surface dry to touch before watering.

**DIRECT LIGHT**

❖ Century Plant

Century plant- Prefers infrequent watering, soil dry to touch before watering.

❖ Citrus Plant

Citrus plant- Prefers frequent watering, keep soil moist.

❖ Corn Plant (can be grown in indirect bright light)

Corn plant-Prefers infrequent watering, soil surface dry to touch before watering.

❖ Croton Plant

Croton plant- Prefers frequent watering, keep soil moist.

❖ Dumb Cane (can be grown in indirect bright light)

Dumb cane- Prefers infrequent watering, soil dry to touch before watering.

❖ Dwarf Date Palm

Dwarf date palm- Prefers frequent watering, keep soil moist.

❖ English Ivy (can be grown in indirect bright light)

English ivy-Prefers frequent watering, keep soil moist.

❖ Fig Tree

Fig tree- Prefers frequent watering, keep soil moist.

- ❖ Fishtail Palm (can be grown in indirect bright light)

Fishtail palm- Prefers frequent watering, keep soil moist.

- ❖ Lady Palm

Lady palm- Prefers frequent watering, keep soil moist.

- ❖ Prayer Plant

Prayer plant- Prefers frequent watering, keep soil moist.

- ❖ Spider Plant (can be grown in indirect bright light)

Spider plant- Prefers frequent watering, keep soil moist.

- ❖ TI Plant

Ti plant- Prefers infrequent watering, soil dry to touch before watering.

- ❖ Umbrella Plant

Umbrella plant- Prefers frequent watering, keep soil moist.

- ❖ Wandering Jew

Wandering Jew - Prefers infrequent watering, soil dry to touch before watering.

- ❖ Wax Plant

Wax plant- Prefers infrequent watering, soil dry to touch before watering.

- ❖ Yucca Plant

Yucca plant- Prefers infrequent watering, soil dry to touch before watering.

## Flowering Plants

Most indoor flowering plants require direct light to maintain their bloom. However, as with most blooming plants, once the flowers drop especially in winter, there is little chance of new ones blooming. Thereafter, enjoy flowering plants green foliage for ambiance in your home, or heaven forbid! Throw out your plant.

## Flowering Plants for Indoors

❖ Azalea

Azalea- Prefers frequent watering, keep soil moist.

❖ Begonia

Begonia- Prefers frequent watering, keep soil moist.

❖ Chrysanthemum

Chrysanthemum- Prefers frequent watering, keep soil moist.

❖ Cyclamen

Cyclamen- Prefers frequent watering, keep soil moist.

❖ Lilies

Lilies - Prefers frequent watering, keep soil moist.

❖ Poinsettia

Poinsettia- Prefers frequent watering, keep soil moist.

# Watering Your Plants

It would probably be safe to say that everyone knows that plants need water to survive. But not everyone knows exactly when to water, or how much.

Not all plants need the same amount of water or at the same time. Too much water will play havoc on your plants as will too little.

So, when do you water your plants?

Do you have an approach to your plants watering needs?

Well one thing is for certain, we all agree plants need water.

As simple as this may sound, if you don't know your individual plants watering needs, it won't take long for your plant(s) to fade away to nothing more than a dried stick and die. To prevent this from happening, we just need to know a little bit more about how water affects your plants.

This starts with what kind of soil is in the pot, how much to water and when. And, what are the room temperature, humidity, and light levels in your home.

## Plant Soil

When you buy a house plant, it is usually growing in a potting soil mixture of peat moss, vermiculite, and perlite. This growing medium nourishes the plants roots by retaining nutrients and creating small air pockets in the soil. Because this soil mixture is loose and airy, water will drain quickly through the mixture leaving just the right amount of moisture behind to be absorbed by the plants roots.

To prevent access water from forming a puddle on your floor or carpet, place the plant pot in a catch-tray or saucer that is large enough to retain the water overflow. And, don't forget to remove any buildup of water in the catch-tray, especially if the pot holes sit in water.

Because this growing medium is so plant friendly, I strongly recommend that when purchasing potting soil for transplanting; make sure the soil includes the growing mixture.

**When to Water**

Before you water your plants, first check to see if the soil feels dry to the touch. If it feels dry, insert a finger into the soil approximately two inches deep and if it still feels dry, then it is time to water your plant.

Another popular method for testing soil moisture is using a soil moisture meter. You can purchase one at most garden centers or at your local nursery for a very reasonable price. Both of these methods work quite well to make sure your plants have enough moisture in the soil, however to keep your plants healthy, you must test the soil for moisture on a regular schedule.

## Humidity

The frequency when to water your plants will vary throughout the season due to humidity change. Winter is the time of year with the least amount of humidity in your home causing increased moisture evaporation from your plants soil; therefore you will need to water your plants more frequently.

Another suggestion and one I definitely recommend is placing a humidifier in the near proximity of your plant(s). The use of a humidifier will dramatically increase the humidity in a room and slow down soil moisture evaporation. It will also help those plants whose leaves depend on high humidity to stay healthy.

Here is a thought, if you have a large room with many plants and don't want to invest in more than one humidifier. Place a bowl almost full with water near your plant for added humidity. Also, don't forget to add water to the bowl as it evaporates. And, because you love your plants, why not purchase a thermometer that also shows a humidity reading. I have seen many at garden outlets for around ten dollars.

While writing about humidity, another thought came into my mind that is worth mentioning. Because the sun is most intense in summer, any plants that receive sun through your windows will experience an increase in the loss of soil moisture. Get to know your plants room location and be sure to check moisture loss more frequently for those plants that are exposed to long hours of sunlight.

## Temperature

Even though we love our indoor plants, it has been my experience that most home owners will set the thermostat for their own comfort level during cold temperatures and air conditioning set to a personal comfort level during the summer months. And, no one including me can argue with that. However, there are some things that can be done to help your plants to stay healthy.

Locate all plants away from heating or a/c vents or dry and drafty areas, and place your plant pot in a catch-tray or container filled with water. Add enough pebbles to the catch-tray or container so that the pot holes remain above the water line.

## Salt

I cannot say it any clearer than this. Plants do not like salt! And, it is probably something you would never think about when tending your plants.

Your plants get soluble salt from fertilizer, but mostly from the water you use when you water them. Depending on where you live, some areas of the country have more soluble salt in drinking water than other areas of the country. Yes, even well water is contaminated due to salt leaching from the soil.

The first indication of a salt build up in the plants soil is usually a white powdery film on the soil surface, or you might notice a white crust on the pot rim or around the pot drainage holes.

Overtime, salt build-up can lead to root damage and quite possibly be absorbed into the plants stem causing stunted growth, or leaves turning brown and crusty at the edge. Finally there will be a general wilting of the plant.

To prevent this problem from occurring, if it is too cold outside, place your plant in the kitchen sink and water thoroughly to flush out any residual water retained by the root system. Let the plant stand in the sink until most of the excess water drains through the pot holes before you move it to the catch-tray or plant container.

Make sure you remove old water that may still be in the catch tray and replace the old pebbles with new ones that are not contaminated with salt. Add fresh water in the tray for added plant moisture, but not enough water to enter the pot holes when the plant is sitting on the pebbles. Following these steps will prevent further salt contamination of plant roots.

If you're feeling a little rich these days, salt build up in the plants soil will not happen if you water using only distilled water.

# What Plants Like

If your plant is stressed in any way; if it's getting too much water, if it's not getting enough light, etc., just know that it's much more susceptible to pests, diseases and viruses. We're going to start with basic principles for plant care.

## Water

When it comes to interior plants, water is my favorite topic, because most people do it way too often. Once a week, sometimes less, is all indoor plants really need. You want the top quarter to half of the soil to feel dry before you water again. Remember, the roots travel downward towards the bottom of the pot.

I water my plants every ten to fourteen days, depending on how they look. I've been working with and enjoying houseplants for so long that it's instinctual for me. You might want to schedule watering for every Sunday so you don't over do it. If that top portion of the soil is still moist, then skip it for at least a few days. Put it in your calendar so you can keep track.

You want the water to run all the way through the plant, but have no more than a quarter to half inch accumulate in the saucer. If there's too much water in the saucer the roots can rot out.

healthy roots = healthy plants

Roots are the foundation of the plant and they need oxygen to breath. If you water your plants too much, then you're depriving the roots of the oxygen they need.

**Here are some important things to know when it comes to watering:**

- Use room temperature water. We wouldn't like ice cold or boiling hot water poured on us either.
- Speaking of ice cold, don't dump your ice cubes into your houseplants.
- The larger the pot, the more soil it holds and the slower it will dry out.
- Plants in lower light dry out slower and need less water.
- If the top of the soil is still moist, resist the urge to water it even though it's been ten days since the last watering.
- If the soil of your plant's pot is covered with moss or rocks, it will dry out slower.
- Different plants will dry out faster or need more water than other plants.
- Water your houseplants less often in the winter, because it's a slower growth time. Back off with the liquid love because they like to rest a bit.
- Put your plants out in the rain to flush out some of the buildup in the soil. Make sure it's not a cold, hard, driving

rain. Tie them to something if you can so they don't blow over. It's a great way to clean off the foliage too.

- If the soil smells or you see tiny flies (fungus gnats), your plant is too wet.

- Don't keep saucers full of water. Remember, you don't want the roots to rot out.

- If your plant has totally dried out, this is one time you want to soak it well. Water it in a pail or saucer and let the roots drink that water up for fifteen minutes. Don't water it every day, but let it come back up to its prior happy condition and then resume watering it as needed.

## Guidelines for Watering

These guidelines can be applied to all plants. You'll find a link back to this page on each plant page in the "List of Plants" section.

I wish I could tell you "water your Pothos every six days" and "water your Rubber Plant every eight days" but it's not that cut and dry. Watering amounts will vary depending on the plant and pot size, as well as the temperature, lighting and humidity in your home. Most plants in this book have an average to low need for water.

**Average**: Water when the top quarter to half of the soil is dry. Water every one to two weeks.

**Low**: Allow the top half of the soil to dry out. Water every two to three weeks.

**Lower than low**: No more than every three weeks. Succulents fall into this category and know that you will kill them fast if they are kept too wet.

If you throw both hands up in the air when it comes to watering houseplants but still want a little greenery in your nice cozy home, here are a few things you should consider:

**A moisture meter**:  I've never used one, but there are a variety of them on the market. They tell you when to water your plants.

**A Watering App**: It reminds you when to water your plants. This one is free so it's worth checking out: Waterbot: Plants Watering.

**Self-watering pots**: You can find different styles and colors to suit your decor.


Self-watering inserts and reservoirs: These go inside the decorative pot. With these last two options, you keep the reservoirs full and the plants drink up the water as they need it.

**Light**

Light is essential to all plants; they need it to photosynthesize. Simply put, this is the process by which they use sunlight to the make food that makes them green. Then they give off oxygen - we want that. One of the keys to the survival of your plants is finding the right amount of light they need.

Most houseplants in this book like bright light but nothing direct or scorching for hours on end. In their native environments, most of them grow under the canopies of trees. The greenhouses they're grown in are glass, fiberglass or plastic but are whitewashed or shade clothed to filter out the strong sun.

Many plants will adapt to lower light situations but will grow much slower. If your plant isn't getting enough light, the growth will be leggy and spindly. The leaves could be smaller, appear less green, and may turn yellow. If the light is too strong, the leaves will burn and you'll see large brown dry patches. They could look parched or faded but too much light might actually be the culprit.

- Rotate your plants every now and then. They grow towards the light because they need it to produce chlorophyll, which is what keeps them green. Nobody wants to tan on only one side!
- Plants are like people - they like it dark at night to sleep. This is why some of the plants in commercial environs can suffer. Make sure your lights are turned off for at least six hours so your plants get the shuteye they need.
- Move your plants a bit throughout the seasons. They might need this as the light changes. A few inches can make a big difference.
- Don't have your plants up against glass. Ouch - this will burn them. On the other hand, cold glass can do damage too.

## Guidelines for Light

These guidelines can be applied to all plants. You'll find a link back to this page on each plant page in the "List of Plants" section.

These will vary a bit depending on the number of windows you have, trees shading your house, and if you keep your curtains or blinds closed. Use your common sense to figure it out. Your plants will let you know if they're happy or not.

**High Light**: Southern exposure with five to six hours of direct sun coming in the windows every day. Make sure your plants are a good distance from the windows or they'll burn. In most cases, high light doesn't mean hot, direct sun. As a rule, the higher the light and the warmer the temps, the more water your plant will need. Western exposure in combo with southern exposure is brightest.

**Medium Light**: Western or eastern exposure with three hours of direct sun coming in the windows every day. Southern exposure would be okay too if the plant was a good distance from the window. Six to eight hours of bright light would fit the bill too.

**Low Light:** Northern exposure with no direct sun coming in the windows. All day electric lighting would be fine too. Know that low light is not no light.

These next few paragraphs are a quick summarization of how to supplement light levels. If your lighting is adequate, then skip right on to temperature.

**Natural light** is best for houseplants but oftentimes our homes just don't have enough of it. And, as ruled by Mother Nature, there's less of it in the winter. It's important to know that high and medium light plants need natural light. The mix of fluorescent and incandescent lighting that I will be referring to below is for low light plants and low to medium light plants only.

Fluorescent lighting gives plants the blue light they need. Most of us don't think that tube lighting is too attractive or appealing. We wouldn't want to hook a fluorescent light system up in our homes so it's good to know that CFL (compact fluorescent lights) bulbs exist. These just screw into a standing or tabletop light fixture which takes at least a hundred-watt bulb. How many you need depends on how low your light levels are.

Houseplants also need red light which is provided by incandescent lights. You want a nice balance of both fluorescent and incandescent light, in a ratio of two to one. Be sure not to leave your lights on all night. Even plants in low light situations require at least six hours of darkness.

**Temperature;**

I'm not going into detail about this but, if your home is comfortable to you, then it should be so for your plants too. The greenhouses that they're grown in are also air conditioned and heated to keep the temperature relatively constant.

**Humidity;**

The plants in this book, succulents aside, really like humidity. Most homes, unless you live in the desert, offer decent enough humidity. There are ways to increase humidity if you think you must.

You can buy a humidifier; there are actually some tabletop models on the market. Another way to increase humidity is to spray the plant with water, but that gets a little labor intensive. Plus, your floor may not be very happy if you do it every day. Glasses of water can be put around the plant or tucked inside the decorative container. Lastly, trays or saucers filled with pebbles and water will help. Just make sure the grow pot does not sit directly in the water.

## Air Circulation

Remember, these plants are grown in greenhouses with fans and vents to the outside world. They do like air from the great outdoors, but the plants in this book were used in office environments with recycled air and little circulation. Most of them had a good survival rate.

* When the weather warms up, be sure to open your windows if you can.

* Keep plants out of tight corners and places with little natural air and circulation.

* A ceiling fan or small fan will help circulate the air in your home if need be.

Fertilizing

I'm not big on fertilizers for plants in the garden, but I do believe in them for houseplants. The soil gets "old" after a while and loses nutrients. However, resist the urge to do it too often. Salts from the fertilizers can build up in the soil and you don't want that. A white crust will form on the soil, the ends of the leaves will look burned and damage can be done to the roots.

If that happens, be sure and take your plant to the sink, tub, or outside to give it a good flushing. If you water has a lot of salts in it, this will be an ongoing problem.

Over fertilizing is as bad as if not worse than over watering. You will burn the roots of your plants.

Fertilizing twice a year is usually enough and should only be done during the active growing season, which is Spring through late Summer.

- Use an organic fertilizer that you water in.
- Use the fertilizer at less than the recommended dose. That way you won't overdo it.
- Never fertilize plants when they are bone dry. Water first, wait five to seven days and then fertilize. You don't want to stress the plant or burn the roots.
- Two organic houseplant fertilizers to try:
- Organics Rx Indoor Plant Food
- Houseplants Alive!

## Cleaning

Plants are like people. We all like to be clean. The dust and dirt that builds up on the leaves can block their pores. Plants need to breath, and if you keep them clean, they'll look better too.

If you can't take them outside or want to do it in the colder months, then use a damp, soft towel or rag to wipe down plants with larger leaves. The method works great for plants like Dracaena Janet Craig, Ficus lyrate and Aspidistra.

You can also use a spray bottle filled with room temperature water and mist the heck out of them. A little white vinegar plus a few drops of a mild dish soap added will help with the cleaning. If this is going to be long, drawn out process then be sure to cover the surface of your plant's soil so it doesn't get drenched. And, be sure to protect your floors because the soap will be slippery or could damage them.

There are some natural leaf shines out there, as well as recipes to make your own, but I don't think they are necessary.

Some additional cleaning tips to keep in mind:

- Never use oils to clean and polish your plants.
- If your plants are really dusty and dirty, consider use a soft brush or soft toothbrush (for smaller plants) to give them a good cleaning.
- Clean on a regular basis so the grime doesn't build up.
- A rain shower is a great way to clean your plants.

- Jades and Aloes don't like cleaning in the winter. Take them outside and give them a good hose down when the weather warms up.

## Pruning

I love to prune and must admit that I'm a bit of a maniac with the Felcos in my garden. However, I very rarely prune my houseplants, because there's rarely a need. There are a few reasons why you may need to do it, and if one of them arises, just make sure your pruners or scissors are very clean and sharp. You can find a blog post and a video tutorial showing how to clean and sharpen your pruners on my website.

### Reasons to prune:

- Remove brown tips caused by salts in the water, dry air or irregular watering.
- Thin out leaves, stems or branches, whether it be for aesthetic reasons or for the health of the plant.
- Control shape
- Restrict height
- Propagation

## Soil

Many plants come from the growers planted with a good amount of crushed, dark orange lava rock or perlite mixed in. This aids with drainage and keeps them from rotting out. You don't want your plant in heavy soil. When you need to transplant it, be sure to use a good, organic potting soil. Make sure it specifies on the bag that it's suitable for indoor plants or houseplants.

Jade plants, snake plants, and aloes must have soil with excellent drainage to keep them on the dry side. You can use the same potting soil that you would for the other plants in this book, but be sure to keep them very dry. You can also add some small crushed rock, perlite, or horticultural sand to lighten the soil and amend the drainage. Or, you can buy a mix that is specially formulated for cactus and succulents.

- Just be sure not to use a regular planting mix, because it's way too heavy for houseplants.
- The soil needs to drain. Make sure the pot they're growing in has drain holes.

## Repotting

The rule to follow is this: the more a plant grows, the larger a pot it will need to accommodate the root growth. Think of it like this: children need bigger shoes as their bodies get bigger. Houseplants do grow slower than plants in the garden, so don't feel the need to repot every year.

I increase the size of a pot about every three years and only go up one pot size. Use your common sense when transplanting. If a plant is eight feet tall and crammed in a ten inch pot then you could easily go to a fourteen inch grow pot.

Here's how I do it: lay down a sheet or tarp to protect the floor. Then run a knife or pruning saw, depending on the circumference of the pot, around the very edge of the root ball to loosen it away from the pot. Chances are it won't just fall out easily, so squeeze the pot to help it on its way. I've had to step on (gently - no lead foot stomping here) and rotate the pots of floor plants to get them out. If all else fails, cut the grow pot away if you can.

Cover the drain holes of the new pot with pieces of coffee filters. This keeps the fresh, loose soil you'll add in from falling right out. You could use a layer of newspaper for this because it works just fine too.

Eyeball the depth, or height, of the root ball to so see how much soil needs to be dumped into the bottom of the pot. You can measure the root ball and then measure inside the pot if this works better for you.

At this point, you can water that soil in so it compacts down. Add more soil in to build it back up if needed. I tend to do this step dry and then water it all at once at the end. I leave the root ball up an extra inch or so because the weight of the root ball will pull it down. How much you leave it up depends on the

# What Plants Don't Like

## Pests

I'll start this section off with pests, buggies and insects. Call them what you please, but your plant may get an infestation at some point. Houseplants are subject to many pests, the most common being mealy bugs and spider mites. I'm touching lightly on this subject because, hopefully, you won't ever have to deal with them, or if you do, you'll catch them in the early stages. Most pests can be treated with the same remedies. If you refer to this section, at least you'll be informed as to what the pest is and what to do for it.

Below are the insects I've seen most commonly infesting houseplants, so keep your eye out for:

### Mealybugs

These tiny white insects actually leave behind a trail that looks like little pieces of cotton. The males have wings. Mealy bugs especially like to hang out in the nodes and the undersides of the leaves. Your plant can become sticky because of the substance they secrete. Also, there are root mealy bugs which dwell in the soil on the roots of the plant. They are hard to detect and even harder to control. Just because your plant has

## Whiteflies

These look exactly like their name - small white flies. They're usually found underneath the leaves. We used to get them in our greenhouse.

## Fungus Gnats

These small, dark flies hatch in the soil. They don't damage the plants, but can be an annoyance to you. No worries though, because they don't bite. They are short lived, but lay a lot of eggs. Let the soil dry out as much as it will take.

## Thrips

I've seen infestations of thrips many times on outdoor plants, but rarely on those indoors. They're teeny tiny, black-winged insects and cause splotching on the leaves. When the infestation gets bad, the leaf takes on a silvery sheen. Be sure to check the undersides of the leaves, because like other buggies, that's where they tend to dwell.

My houseplants have fortunately lived their little green lives pest free so far. I'm an organic gardener so if needed, I would treat them with rubbing alcohol or vinegar, with a few drops of mild dish soap added in. Be careful with these. Even though they are natural remedies, if you use too strong a concentration, you can burn the plant.

If you catch pests in the early stages, then you can take the plant to the sink or shower and give it a spray off. The succulents in my garden get aphids and I have at it with the garden hose to get rid of them. Be sure to get in the nodes and the under sides of the leaves too.

**Remedies**:

* Apple Cider Vinegar. One tablespoon per pint spray bottle along with two drops of dish soap. Fill with water.
* Rubbing Alcohol. One eighth to one quarter cup per pint spray bottle along with two drops of dish soap. Fill with water.

* Sticky Yellow Traps. Good for flying insects like whiteflies and fungus gnats. You can find them online here.
* Blue Sticky Traps. Good for thrips control. You can find them online here.

* Neem Oil is considered a natural insecticide and fungicide. Many people swear by it for getting rid of pests on houseplants. If you want to try Neem, you can find it online here.
* Insecticidal soap and horticultural oil. You can also purchase insecticidal soap or horticultural oil, but I think it's just as easy to make your own. This is important: if you're using any of the

above three, just make sure what you are buying is safe to use on houseplants and apply only at the recommended ratios. A bad infestation doesn't mean you should increase the ratio.

Methods:

* Washing or Hosing

* Spraying. A hand-held sprayer in whatever size fits your needs. Unless you have a lot of plants, a pint-size one will do the trick.

* Wiping Down. Use a soft, damp rag to wipe the leaves off. You can dunk it into a pail with dish soap and a little cider vinegar if you have a lot of leaves to do. Don't use that cloth on non-infested plants until you thoroughly clean it.

* Q-Tip or Cotton Ball. Dip the tip or ball in a mixture of one-to-one alcohol to water and dab it on the insect. This method is good for mealybugs and scale. Growing up we had a home greenhouse and this was the method my dad had me use for getting the upper hand on mealybugs on our giant Jade plant.

* Hand Picking. This works on scale.

Drenching. This works on fungus gnat larvae still living in the soil. As said above, make sure you let the soil completely dry first. Mix one tablespoon apple cider vinegar per gallon of water and use it to water the infected plant a you normally would for three to four watering cycles

This is important: if the insect infestation is bad, it's best to bid the plant adieu. Repeated treatments will weaken the plant or the insects could build up immunity to whatever you're using. Besides, who wants to spend all their free time treating plants? Send it to the great compost bin in the sky and start with a fresh, new plant. Your other plants will thank you!

Other things to know about pests:

* Make sure any houseplants you're buying and bringing home are insect free. They're tightly displayed at the nursery or garden center making it easy for the critters to travel from plant to plant.

* If your plants have been enjoying the warmer months outdoors, then be sure to hose them off well before bringing indoors. This prevents buggy hitchhikers which will become a problem fast.

* Treat when you first see signs of insects. You have a much better chance of getting the upper hand if you do this. Like anything, the longer you wait to treat, the worse it will get.

* Pests in general love the tender, juicy new growth (it's oh so easy to chew on and suck the good stuff out of) so be sure to check it from time to time.

* It is very important to treat the undersides of the leaves too. Buggies love to breed and hang out there. It's a good place for them to hide from you. You might need to get a magnifying glass to see them.

* If you see a black substance on your houseplants that looks like soot, it's the residue left behind by aphids, mealybugs, scale or whiteflies.

* Insects particularly like it when you turn your heat on, so keep your eye out for them at that time.

* You will have to do repeated treatments at seven to ten day intervals for four weeks to get the insects under control.

* If one plant is infested, isolate it from your other plants during the treatment period.

* Keep the leaves of your houseplants clean.

* Plants with fuzzy leaves don't like being sprayed.

Other Things Houseplants Don't Like:

* Direct heat. Don't place plants on or close to heaters. Even though they like warmer temperatures, a heater will fry them. If you don't like it, your plants won't either.

* Air conditioners. On the other end of the spectrum, they don't like being in front of blowing cold air. Brrrr.

* Drafty windows and doors. Good air circulation is necessary, but a cold draft doesn't qualify as that.

* Hot, strong sunlight. Light is necessary, but too much hot sun is sure to burn your plants.

* Deep, dark corners. All plants need some light, even if it's artificial, and as I mentioned above, they need air circulation too.

* Smoke. Cough, cough. It's not good for us and it's not good for your plants either.

* Dust. Plants breathe through their leaves and a buildup of too much dust will hinder that. We want that wonderful oxygen they give off.

* Too much water. I've said it before, but it's worth repeating. Don't empty your glass into a plant every time you have something left in it. You might like soda, beer, or juice, but plants don't. Make sure water is not accumulating in their saucers.

* Ice. Don't dump it in your houseplants. Remember, they're native to the tropics not the polar Arctic. They don't like freezing water. It could also lead to houseplant public enemy #1: overwatering.

* Kitties. Some of them love to chew on the crunchy leaves of some plants. However, both kitties and houseplants can cohabit peacefully in your home together. I have two cats and one of them will munch on my plants while the other doesn't pay any attention to them at all. Oscar is particularly fond of the Dracaena marginata and my Bromeliad, so both have been moved to spots he can't get to. Buying some cat grass would be

an option too. I've also heard that some like to play in the dirt. You might want to consider covering the pot's surface with moss, stones or glass chips to keep Fluffy from digging.

# Easiest to Grow Houseplants

Growing and creating fresh air in your home or office doesn't have to be difficult. Many houseplants do not require a lot of care, sunlight, or water. If you have a brown thumb rather than a green one, the plants in this chapter are a good place to start.

All the plants in this chapter are hardy plants that are easy to take care of and can withstand neglect. Most of these plants only require watering a maximum of once per week, many less frequently than that. Most of these plants also do well in low lighting or shade, which makes them great for interiors, especially office buildings where there may not be many windows for natural light.

Each plant is listed with a picture of the plant for reference, an explanation of the toxins it cleans from the air, maintenance instructions, and toxicity to children and pets. This information should be sufficient to allow you to decide the best plants to choose for your home or office, based on your personal situation.

The NASA studies on indoor pollution done in 1989 recommends 15 to 18 plants in 6 to 8-inch- diameter containers to clean the air in an average 1,800 square foot house. That's roughly one plant per 100 square feet of floor space. This will apply to most plants described below.

# Pigmy Date Palm (Phoenix Robeline)

The pygmy date palm is native to tropical areas of Asia. However, you can easily find them in nurseries around the globe. The pygmy date palm removes several toxins from the air including formaldehyde, xylene, and toluene. The pygmy date palm can survive in low sunlight, and through moderate drought conditions. This means that it is suitable for indoors and does not have to be by a window. Typically, pygmy date palms stay adequately moist if you water them once each week.

This plant is non-toxic for children and pets. Pruning pygmy palm trees is sometimes necessary to keep its growth manageable, especially in smaller settings. Pygmy palm growing is used in a variety of interiors capes and commercial plantings due to its graceful form and height of 6 to 10 feet. When grown in soil with a pH over 7, the tree may develop potassium or magnesium deficiency.

## Boston Fern (Nephrolepisexaltata)

The Boston fern is a common houseplant and does well in indirect light. Native to tropical climates of South America, Florida, and Africa, this plant does require frequent watering. However, it is somewhat resistant to drought, so forgetting to water it for a few days will not harm it.

The best indoor temperature range for these voluptuous plants is between 68 F and 78 F

It does require high humidity to thrive, so if your humidity is below 80%, you should mist it with water frequently. If you wish to avoid misting, pair the Boston Fern in a room with a plant that expels water into the air, such as an areca palm. The Boston fern cleans the air of formaldehyde, xylene, and toluene and can be grown in either a pot or hanging basket. This plant is non-toxic to children and pets.

**Kimberley Queen Fern (Nephrolepis obliterate)**

The Kimberley Queen fern is not as well-known as the Boston fern, but is very similar in many respects, including appearance. Originating in Australia, this plant is easily found in garden centers and nurseries. It is not as sensitive to humidity as the Boston fern, so it does not have to be frequently misted. Allow the top two or three inches of soil to dry out before watering again. The fronds of a Kimberly Queen turn a pale green when the plant needs water. Crispy brown fronds, especially in the center of the plant, indicate too much water. A Kimberly Queen does well in temperatures between 60-85 degrees. If the temperature goes below 60, this fern won't die but it will stop growing.

Like the Boston fern, the Kimberley Queen fern filters formaldehyde, xylene, and toluene from the air. This plant is non-toxic to children and pets.

## Spider Plant (Chlorophytum Como sum)

The spider plant is one of the easiest houseplants to grow in your home for fresh air. It survives in a variety of climates and is resistant to drought. It does best with indirect sunlight. The spider plant cleans the air of formaldehyde, xylene, and toluene, and it is non-toxic to children and pets.

Caring for spider plants is easy. These resilient plants tolerate lots of abuse, making them excellent candidates for new gardeners or those without a green thumb. Provide them with well-drained soil and bright, indirect light and they will flourish. Water them well but do not allow the plants to become too soggy, which can lead to root rot. In fact, spider plants prefer to dry out some between watering. When caring for spider plants, also take into account that they enjoy cooler temperatures — around 55 to 65 F

If you begin to notice spider plant leaves browning, there's no need to worry. Browning of leaf tips is quite normal and will not harm the plant.

**Devil's Ivy (Epipremnumaureum)**

Devil's ivy is so called because it is virtually impossible to kill. This makes it a great houseplant for people who do not do well caring for plants. It requires little care and attention, simply water it occasionally. Devil's ivy cleans the air of benzene, formaldehyde, xylene, and toluene. All portions of devil's ivy are toxic if consumed, so keep the plant well out of the reach of children and pets. Also keep in mind that because some people have an allergic reaction to the sap, you should consider wearing gloves when you're pruning the plant.

Indoor Ivy typically range from 6 to 8 feet in length if left unpruned. The vine produces waxy, heart-shaped foliage variegated with bright yellow and green, the size of the leaves depends on where the plant is cultivated. Indoors, the leaves may reach about 4 inches in length. If you're growing it in containers, an all-purpose, peaty potting mix that drains well is adequate for proper growth.

Situate the plant an area that receives filtered sunlight or bright artificial light for optimal growth. You should water houseplants deeply — until it runs from the bottom drainage holes — approximately once a week or when the top inch or two of soil feels dry. During winter, cut back on watering to about once every other week.

## Chinese Evergreen (Aglaonema modestum)

The Chinese evergreen is a very easy houseplant to care for. It thrives well in low light conditions and does not require frequent watering. This makes it ideal for people who do not have a lot of time to spend caring for plants. The Chinese evergreen filters the air of benzene and formaldehyde. This plant is highly toxic to children and pets. A dermatological reaction is common when touching the plant's crystals.

Chinese evergreen plants thrive in medium to low light conditions, or indirect sunlight. These plants prefer temperatures no lower than 60 F. (16 C.) with average indoor temps ranging between 70-72 F.

Chinese evergreens require an evenly moist soil environment and high humidity. Aglaonema cannot tolerate dry air, so water the plant until the soil is moderately moist. Allow a bit of drying out between watering as heavy or excessive watering may lead to fungal problems such as stem or root rot.

# Selloum philodendron (Philodendron bipinnatifidum)

A Philodendron Selloum or Tree Philodendron is native to South America, but also grows outdoors on the East and Gulf coasts of the United States. Indoors, the easy-care, self-heading Philodendron Selloum takes up a lot of space, often spreading 5ft. or more with 2ft.-3ft. leaves. The dark green, shiny leaves are large and deeply lobed. A Selloum does grow a trunk as it matures, but the huge drooping leaves usually hide it.

These plants are considered toxic and should be kept away from pets and children.

The selloum philodendron is a hearty tropical plant from South America. In its natural habitat, it has lots of direct sunlight, so it does adapt well to a shaded environment. It does not require frequent watering, but you may need to occasionally trim it back as it grows. This houseplant cleans the air of formaldehyde.

**Elephant Ear Plant (Philodendron domesticum)**

The elephant ear plant is another of the philodendron family, which is a hearty family of plants that can withstand neglect. It only needs to be watered when the soil becomes dry, and it does not need to be in direct sunlight.

This houseplant will clean the air of formaldehyde and is highly toxic to pets and kids. It does not do well in hanging baskets, so if you have small pets or children, keep it on a high shelf or choose from one of the other many options for growing fresh air.

Grow elephant ears in moist, loamy soil with a high organic matter content. They are easy to maintain once you get them going.

## Snake Plant (Sansevieria trifasciata)

The snake plant is an extremely easy houseplant to care for. It

tolerates low light very well and can be placed virtually anywhere in the home.

The snake plant also tolerates infrequent watering and prefers less water, as soggy soil leads to rotting roots. The snake plant is one of the best for air purification. It exchanges carbon dioxide for oxygen using a crassulacean acid metabolism process not common in many plants. It will also purify your air of benzene, formaldehyde, trichloroethylene, xylene, and toluene. This plant is toxic to children and pets.

Snake plants do best with a free-draining soil mix, because they are easily prone to rot. Allow soil to dry between watering and take extra special care not to over water in winter. Try to avoid getting leaves wet when you water.

## Red Edged Dracaena (Dracaena marginata)

The red edged dracaena is a great houseplant because it requires little attention. It does best in filtered or indirect sunlight and tolerates infrequent watering.

The red edges of this easy dracaena bring a pop of color, and the shrub can grow to reach your ceiling. This plant is best for removing xylene, trichloroethylene and formaldehyde, which can be introduced to indoor air through lacquers, varnishes and gasoline.

Temperature shifts may cause those red-edged leaves to yellow and even die back. The perfect temperature for your plant is between 60 to 70 degrees Fahrenheit during the day and 50 to

60 degrees at night. Take care not to position a potted Dracaena near a heater or a window that allows in chilly breezes.

There are many dracaena plants. This distinctive version is distinguished by the purple-red edges on its ribbon-like green leaves. Although it grows slowly, it can eventually get as high as 15 feet tall, so perhaps put it in a room with high ceilings and moderate sunlight. This plant is toxic to children and pets.

**Dumb Canes (Dieffenbachia)**

Dumb Canes is a good houseplant that requires moderate care. The soil does need to be kept moist as well as a moderate amount of filtered sunlight, such as from a nearby window. This houseplant doesn't filter very many toxins, only doing a good job of canceling out xylene and toluene. However, it will help generate clean oxygen for your home.

This plant is extremely toxic to children and pets. The sap of the plant is acrid, and when ingested can numb the throat and vocal cords, rendering the victim mute for up to two weeks until the poison wears off. The sap is highly irritating to the skin, and any interactions with the plant which result in sap exposure should be washed thoroughly.

Maybe consider this plant for an adult household with no kids or pets.

## Janet Craig (Dracaena deremensis)

The Janet Craig house plant is a great plant that requires very little care. It is very tolerant of neglect, does not require a lot of water, and can thrive in any type of lighting.

Most plants grown for interior use are 10-inch pots with 3 plants per pot, ranging in height of 24-32 inches. Some 14-inch pots are grown as well with 4 plants per pot and reach a height of 30-42 inches.

Dracaena deremensis cultivars do not like heat. This is very important to remember especially during summer months when plants have a tendency to discolor.

Recommended maximum temperature is 90 degrees. As temperatures increase above 95 degrees, problems with leaf discoloring and leaf notching may develop.

This houseplant filters the air of benzene, formaldehyde, and trichloroethylene. This plant is highly toxic to children and pets.

**Parlor Palm (Chamaedorea elegans)**

The parlor palm is a very good choice for a houseplant if you like the idea of tree-like plants but don't want something that will grow very large. The parlor palm will only reach a height of about three feet maximum. It is a popular houseplant because it is extremely easy to care for.

Growing a parlor palm tree indoors is ideal because it grows very slowly and thrives in low light and cramped space. Water your indoor parlor palm sparingly – underwatering is better than overwatering. Allow the soil to begin to dry between watering, and water even less in the winter.

If you're planting a parlor palm tree indoors, opt for a few plants in the same container. Individual plants grow straight up and look more attractive and filled out in a group. Parlor palm houseplants have relatively weak root systems and don't mind crowding, so don't transplant more often than necessary.

Parlor Palm Plant Care. Temperature: Average warmth 65°F (18°C) and above is fine and no less than 50°F (10°C) at night.

It does best in low light rooms away from windows, and with infrequent watering. It is also preferred to many other tree-like houseplants because it is non-toxic to dogs, cats, and children. The parlor palm, like other palms, will clean the air of benzene, formaldehyde, and carbon monoxide.

# Swiss Cheese Plant (Monstera deliciosa)

The Swiss cheese plant is a houseplant with large, bushy leaves. It can grow up to two to three feet tall at maturity with good growth conditions. It is a good houseplant to have because it is low maintenance.

The Swiss cheese vine plant prefers full sun but will adapt to partial shade. It also enjoys a moist, well-drained soil. This plant grows best in warm conditions and requires high humidity.

Monstera needs lots of space: Put it in an open environment spot in the living room, rather than in a tight corner or on a windowsill.

Monstera can grow up trees and other plants in the rainforest, and would benefit from some support indoors, too. Consider adding a small trellis or pole nearby.

If you can't commit to a whole Monstera plant—or if yours is running rampant—trim a leaf or two and stand them upright in a clear glass vase.

The plant needs warm interior temperatures of at least 65 degrees Fahrenheit (18 C.) or warmer. Swiss cheese plant also needs moderately moist soil and high humidity

The Swiss cheese plant was not part of the original study done by NASA. However, it is a good houseplant to have for air quality because it will eliminate carbon dioxide and add humidity to the air. This plant is toxic to children and pets.

# Neem Tree (Azadirachta indica)

The neem tree is a great addition to your home. It is very easy to care for, requiring bright sunlight and weekly watering for moist soil. The neem tree is well known for its medicinal properties, which should be used with caution due to some potential side effects, primarily for women. The plant should not be idly ingested by children or pets. The neem tree is one of the best plants to absorb carbon dioxide and release oxygen into the air, although it has not been studied for its effects on other air pollutants.

Your neem house plant will initially grow slowly, but once it is a year old it should take off, provided you look after it well enough.

Overwatering is probably the biggest risk for your neem tree. They really can't stand wet feet and can get problems with fungi and root rot. The most important thing for a neem tree is warmth and lots of sunlight. The more of both it gets, the faster it will grow.

Neem tree habitats are naturally hot and dry. The tree can tolerate temperatures up to 122 degrees Fahrenheit, but it cannot cope with cold; temperatures below 40 degrees Fahrenheit cause the tree's leaves to fall and can kill the tree. Neem tree's ideal temperature range is around 50 to 98 degrees Fahrenheit.

## Jade Plant (Crassula ovata)

The jade plant has lush, full greenery that is perfect for diluting carbon dioxide in the air and releasing fresh oxygen. It is extremely easy to care for. While it does need plenty of bright indirect sunlight, it does not require frequent watering. It prefers a drier soil, so only water when the top inch of the soil is dry, once every week or two. This plant is non-toxic to children and pets.

Jade plants grow best at room temperature (65 to 75°F) but prefer slightly cooler temperatures at night and in the winter (55°F). Keep soil moist but not wet during active growth in the spring and summer. Allow soil to dry between watering in the winter. Avoid splashing water on the leaves while watering if you can.

**Song of India (Pleomelereflexa)**

The song of India, or Pleomele plant, is a beautiful and easy to grow houseplant. The large leaves and dense foliage make it perfect for generating oxygen and eliminating carbon dioxide in the home. It is a very good plant if you don't have a lot of gardening knowledge. It needs low to medium light and watered only about once a week. It does sometimes require pruning of lower leaves to promote more dense foliage. This plant is slightly toxic to pets.

Like all Dracaenas, the Reflexavariegata likes to be kept on the dry side. Always allow the top 50% of the soil to dry out before watering. High humidity is very helpful for this plant to truly flourish. Basic household temperatures between 65-85 degrees are ideal for the Dracaena Reflexavariegata.

# Additional Plants for Your Home

The plants in this chapter are some of the more exotic and expensive houseplants that you can buy to grow fresh air in your home. Many of these plants are easy to care for but can either be very expensive or grow to be very large. Consider carefully before getting one of these plants for your home. They can be great conversation pieces and well worth the investment if you can care for them.

Some of these plants are trees that get very large, or they are exotic plants that may be harder to find. Some of these plants are harder to care for, and you may need to get further instructions from the providing nursery for the plants' care and growth. A few of the plants are not common as houseplants but can be grown indoors with care.

Again, each plant is listed with a picture for reference, how it purifies the air, toxicity ratings, and instructions for care. This information is provided to help you decide whether you want these plants in your home. You may want to consult the nursery you purchase them for additional information on the more exotic plants.

**Areca Palm (Chrysalidocarpuslutescens)**

The areca palm is native to tropical and subtropical climates but is typically available from most nurseries and garden centers. The adolescent or mature plants can be very expensive, so it is best to get this as a table top plant and grow it to maturity. The areca palm does require sunlight and should be placed near a south or west facing the window. It needs to be watered frequently enough to keep the soil damp. This plant grows about six to ten inches each year until it reaches a height of six to seven feet at its maturity.

You can trim the fronds to keep the plant smaller for use as an indoor plant. It will need to be repotted every two years and has a lifespan of about ten years. Studies have shown that the areca palm cleans the air of formaldehyde, xylene, and toluene.

It also adds humidity to the air, releasing approximately one liter of water every 24 hours. This plant is non-toxic to children and pets.

**Weeping Fig (Ficus benjamina)**

The weeping fig is a tree rather than a traditional houseplant. It does work well as a houseplant because it requires very little care to maintain. It only needs to be watered when the soil becomes dry, and it does well in considerable shade. As a tree, it will need to be pruned or replaced when it grows to considerable size. The weeping fig will cleanse your air of formaldehyde, xylene, and toluene. This plant is toxic to pets.

**King of Hearts (Homalomenawallisii)**

The king of hearts houseplant is common, but hard to care for. It requires a temperate climate that is not cold but also not above 75 degrees. It also requires frequent watering, but the soil cannot be too soggy. This plant is very sensitive and is more easily maintained by someone with a talent for caring for plants. The king of hearts will filter the air of xylene and toluene. This plant is toxic to children and pets.

**Aloe Vera**

Aloe Vera is a very useful houseplant in more ways than one. Although the science is conflicted on the use of Aloe Vera medicinally, it is frequently used to soothe burns and minor cuts. Aloe will also filter the air of benzene and formaldehyde, and it generates oxygen. This houseplant does best in lots of light and potted in a very sandy soil. It does not require a lot of water and needs a pot with good drainage. This plant is toxic to children and pets.

**Dragon Tree (Dracaena marginata)**

The dragon tree is a good houseplant for generating oxygen and filtering the air. It filters the air of benzene, formaldehyde, xylene, and toluene. The dragon tree can grow to be quite tall, generally about six feet in height as a houseplant. It is, however, very easy to maintain. It does not require much water and can survive well in high or low light. It tolerates neglect very well. This plant is toxic to pets.

**Lady Palm (Rhapisexcelsa)**

The lady palm is another tree that you can bring indoors for air quality. This tree is native to sub-tropical climates and does best in a room with higher humidity. If your home has low humidity, you may want to spray the lady palm with a fine mist of warm water every few days. You also want to keep the soil moist, although this houseplant does well in low light or filtered light. The lady palm will filter the air of carbon dioxide, formaldehyde, xylene, and ammonia. This plant is non-toxic to children and pets.

**Red Emerald (Philodendron erubescens)**

The red emerald is a very common and popular houseplant that eradicates toxins from the air. It filters all common harmful toxins, including benzene, formaldehyde, trichloroethylene, xylene, toluene, and ammonia. This houseplant is fairly easy to care for. It does well in low light conditions, but it does better in higher humidity. Keep it watered and occasionally mist if your home is dry. This plant is toxic to children and pets.

**Schefflera (Brassaiaactinophylla)**

The Schefflera, also known as an umbrella tree, is a good houseplant to have for getting rid of toxins and generating oxygen. The Schefflera eliminates benzene, formaldehyde, xylene, and toluene from the air. It requires medium and indirect sunlight and should only be watered when the soil becomes dry. This plant is toxic to children and pets.

**Ficus "Alii" (Ficus maclellandii)**

This small tree is a hybrid that has been cultivated for use as an indoor houseplant. The ficus alii is a good houseplant for removing toxins from the air including benzene, formaldehyde, and trichloroethylene. It is also good for generating oxygen and limiting carbon dioxide. It is very easy to care for and exists well in low light with frequent watering. This plant is toxic to children and pets.

## Dracaena "Warneckei" (Dracaena dermensis)

The Dracaena Warneckei is a tree that can be grown indoors with minimal effort. It is common in office spaces because it does not require frequent watering and it survives well in low light and artificial light. The Warneckei filters the air of benzene and generates oxygen. This plant is toxic to children and pets.

**Syngonium (Syngonium podophyllum)**

The syngonium is a good houseplant to have if you can care for it properly. It requires damp soil, so it must be watered frequently. It also requires either high humidity or daily misting with lukewarm water. It does do well in low light or shade, so it is a good plant for offices and home interiors. The syngonium will filter the air of benzene, formaldehyde, xylene, and toluene. This plant is toxic to children and pets.

## Lacy Tree Philodendron (Philodendron selloum)

The lacy tree philodendron is not as common as other houseplants, but it is a good one for cleaning the air of formaldehyde and carbon dioxide. This houseplant is easy to care for, needing little light and water. However, it does need room to grow, as it can get quite large and bushy. This houseplant is highly toxic to children and pets.

**Norfolk Island Pine (Araucaria heterophylla)**

The Norfolk Island Pine is a tree, but it is not actually a pine at all. This houseplant is most commonly known as the Charlie Brown Christmas tree. However, it is a good houseplant to have in your home year-round. It is very easy to care for, as it does not need frequent watering and it does best in low light conditions. The Norfolk Island Pine will clean the air of formaldehyde, xylene, and toluene. This plant is toxic to children and pets.

**Dwarf Banana (Musa cavendishii)**

The dwarf banana tree is a good addition to your home if you can care for it. It grows to about six feet in height and is great because it is one of the few trees that are grown indoors that are not toxic to pets or children. It will require lots of watering and some sunlight to flourish. The dwarf banana tree will remove formaldehyde from the air and produces a lot of oxygen.

**Croton (Codiaeum variegatum pictum)**

The croton houseplant is not for the faint of heart. This plant will greatly filter the air in your home, eliminating formaldehyde, xylene, and toluene. However, it is extremely difficult to care for. You cannot put this plant in direct sunlight, or the leaves will burn and drop. On the other hand, you cannot have it in a low light room either, or it will wilt. Watering can also be a problem, as too much or too little will kill the plant quickly. However, if you can find the right lighting and watering schedule, this houseplant is a beautiful addition to purify your home. This plant is toxic to children and pets.

**Peacock Plant (Caltheamakoyana)**

The peacock plant is an excellent addition to your home if you like exotic looking houseplants. The markings on the leaves of this plant are exquisite. However, it does take some careful care. You'll need to avoid shady areas, but it also should not be in direct sunlight. It needs small amounts of water daily, and it also requires humidity. If you have a low humidity level in your home, you will need to spray it with water daily. The houseplant does have its merits, however, as it filters the air of xylene and toluene. This plant is non-toxic to children and pets.

**Urn Plant (Aechmea fasciata)**

The urn plant is a very exotic looking houseplant that can be desirable as a conversation piece as well as an air purifier. It requires lots of indirect sunlight. You will have to be very careful about watering this houseplant if you want to keep it in its flowering stage. You'll need to make sure that it does not get too overwatered, but you'll also have to make sure it doesn't get too dry. The urn plant filters the air of xylene, toluene, and ammonia. This plant is non-toxic to children and pets.

**Mass Cane (Dracaena massangeana)**

Mass cane is another indoor tree that makes a good houseplant. Although it can get quite large, it is very slow growing and will fit in a small space for quite some time. Unlike many other indoor trees, the mass cane is easy to care for. It needs only moderate light and only needs to be watered once every one or two weeks. The mass cane, also known as the corn plant, filters trichloroethylene and formaldehyde from the air. While not toxic to humans, mass cane is dangerous for pets such as cats and dogs.

**Ginger (Zingiber officinale)**

Ginger is a plant that is not typically grown indoors, but with some care, it can be a successful houseplant. Ginger is useful in many ways, with the root being a common seasoning. Ginger is also purported to have many health benefits, including reducing inflammation. As a houseplant, ginger will help eliminate carbon dioxide from your home. In addition, it is a great plant for adding humidity to your home. This plant is non-toxic to children and pets.

# Poisonous Plants

The following list of plants is also beneficial for air quality in your home but some are toxic if ingested.

Please pay attention to those plants I do not recommend and make a note of their names to avoid future purchase. Keep this in mind if you have children or pets that may take an interest in tasting any of these plants.

As I am somewhat of an old codger, there's not much in the small children department in my home, but I do have pets which I've noticed show no interest in any of my plants that fall into this group. I'll let you be the best judge regarding inclusion of any of these plants for your home.

A word of advice regarding any plants I list that are toxic. If you have any concern about these plants and whether you should buy them, always, always, check first with your doctor before making a purchase. Let me repeat for those of you who may not be giving full attention to what I just said. Always check with your doctor before purchasing any of these plants that are on the toxic list.

Ok, I'm off my pulpit so let's continue.

I have not included all toxic plants, only the more popular plants that are usually found in the home.

## Agave Plant

Parts that are toxic-

Leaves of this plant contain calcium- oxalate crystals.

Symptoms- leaf spine punctures can cause pain and swelling. Use good gardener's gloves that are spine resistant when handling this plant.

## Angel's Trumpet (Not Recommended)

Parts that are toxic-

All parts of plant.

Symptoms- Dry mouth, muscle weakness, dilated pupils, paralysis, rapid heartbeat, seizures, fever, coma, possible death.

Suggestion- Do not purchase but do remember the name for your do not buy list. Please take note of any toxic plant heading you should not bring home, again, I'll add "not recommended" next to the plants name.

## Asparagus Fern (Not Recommended)

Parts that are toxic-

Berries and contact with plant sap.

Symptoms- Contact with sap may cause skin irritation, swelling, blisters. Eating berries may cause gastrointestinal problems.

Suggestion- If you have small children put this plant on your do not buy list.

## Azalea (Not Recommended)

Not safe for humans or pets.

Eating of this plant may cause symptoms ranging from upset stomach to serious heart and kidney problems.

Suggestion- Do not purchase but do remember the name for your do not buy list.

## Calla Lily (Not Recommended)

Parts that are toxic-

All parts of plant. (Plant contains calcium oxalate crystals).

Symptoms- Burning or swelling of tongue, lips, and throat. Stomach pain, diarrhea, dermatitis, may be fatal to some children.

Suggestion- Definitely do not purchase but do remember the name for your do not buy list.

## Croton

Parts that are toxic

All parts of plant.

Symptoms- May cause skin rash, nausea, vomiting, diarrhea when eaten.

## Desert Rose (Not Recommended)

Parts that are toxic-

All parts of plant.

Symptoms- Plant may cause heart arrhythmia, and nausea. The plant sap is used as arrow poison for hunting in some areas of Africa.

Suggestion- Do not purchase but do remember the name for your do not buy list.

**Devils Ivy**

Parts that are toxic-

Leaves contain calcium oxalate crystals.

Symptoms- May cause swelling of mucous membranes- mouth, tongue, and throat also diarrhea.

**Dracaena (Not Recommended)**

Parts that are toxic-

Poisonous to pets but safe for humans

Suggestion- If you have inquisitive pets, add this plant to your do not buy list.

**Dumb Cane (Dieffenbachia) Not Recommended**

Parts that are toxic-

All parts of plant (contain calcium oxalate crystals).

Symptoms- Swelling of lips, tongue, and throat; difficulty speaking, nausea, vomiting, diarrhea if plant eaten.

Suggestion- If you have inquisitive children that may eat the leaves, add to your do not buy list.

**English Ivy (Not Recommended)**

Parts that are toxic-

Leaves

Symptoms- Plant may cause weeping blisters, difficulty in breathing, vomiting, convulsions, paralysis, and coma.

If you have children, visiting children, or pets, this plant is definitely not recommended for your home.

Suggestion- Do not purchase but do remember the name for your do not buy list.

## Jerusalem Cherry (Not Recommended)

Parts that are toxic-

Plant leaves, unripe berries.

Symptoms- dilated pupils, loss of sensation, vomiting, fever, stomach pain, respiratory problems, may be fatal.

Suggestion- Do not purchase but do remember the name for your do not buy list.

## Oleander (Not Recommended)

It is actually a tree that can grow to 30 feet tall. It is probably one of the most deadliest you will ever encounter. Although quite attractive with white or pinkish blooms I wouldn't wish it on my worst enemy.

Parts that are toxic-

All parts of plant.

Symptoms- Arrhythmia; may cause death, bloody diarrhea, mouth pain, vomiting, nausea, cramps from inhaling burning stems or trunk of tree. The water in a vase that you place cut flowers will become lethal if consumed. This plant is just simply loaded with arsenic in its leaves.

Suggestion- Do not purchase but do remember the name for your do not buy list.

**Pencil Tree (Not Recommended)**

Parts that are toxic- (Plant contains cardiac glycosides).

All parts of plant-

Symptoms- Causes swelling of lips, mouth, and throat, may produce blisters, nausea, vomiting, and diarrhea if eaten.

Suggestion- Put this plant on your do not buy list if you have inquisitive children that may eat the leaves.

**Peace Lily (Not Recommended)**

Parts that are toxic-

Leaves contain calcium oxalate crystals.

Symptoms- Swelling of lips, tongue, throat, may get dermatitis from root sap.

Suggestion- Put this plant on your do not buy list if you have inquisitive children that may eat the leaves

**Philodendron (Not Recommended)**

Parts that are toxic-

All parts of plant (contains calcium oxalate crystals.)

Symptoms- May cause swelling of the lips, tongue, and throat. Difficulty speaking, slurred words, also, nausea, vomiting, and diarrhea.

Suggestion- Put this plant on your do not buy list if you have inquisitive children that may eat the leaves

## Pothos (Devi's Ivy) Not Recommended

Parts that are toxic-

All parts of plant (calcium oxalate crystals)

Symptoms- May cause skin irritation, swelling and burning of lips, mouth, tongue, and throat.

Suggestion- Put this plant on your do not buy list if you have inquisitive children that may eat the leaves

# Care and Maintenance of Your Plants

With the proper care and maintenance, your plants will live longer healthier lives providing you with a green living space. They are also a great tool to teach your children how to care for nature as most kids already have a natural curiosity and will take an interest in their parents' hobbies.

**Top Tips for the Care and Maintenance of Your Houseplants**

**Water**

- Ensure the soil is moist; this can be done by sticking your finger into the soil up to the knuckle to ensure you are down below surface level. The soil should feel damp and your finger should not come away with too much moisture on when you take it out of the soil. If there is excess water the soil is not draining correctly, you will need to check the pot. If it is nice and damp, the plant does not need watering. If it is dry your plant will need water.
- Check for signs and symptoms of over or under watering by looking at the plant's leaves.

**Soil**

- If the soil has mold on it, it is best to re-pot as it may be old and stale. If this is the case it is no longer benefitting the plant.
- If it is soggy it means that there is poor drainage and it is time for new soil. You will have to check the plant's roots for rot or damage.
- There should be no salt buildup on the soil.

- Remember to fertilize the soil regularly.

## Light

- Check what kind of lighting the plant requires.
- Make sure it is positioned in a spot that offers it the most benefit for optimum health.
- If under synthesized lighting conditions make sure that the plant is getting enough time out of the light.

## Fertilizer

- Choose a fertilizer that best suits both your lifestyle and is good for your plants.
- Follow the instructions on the fertilizer with care to ensure your plant is getting the full benefits from the nutrients it has to offer.

## Repotting

- Keep an eye on the plant as it may be outgrowing its current home.
- If potting-up, make sure that the new pot is not too much bigger than the current one. Plants do not like too much space.
- Give the plant time to acclimate to its new environment before filling it with nutrients.

## Maintenance

- Check the plant regularly for pests, diseases, and ailments.
- If there are any signs of a disease or pests isolate the plant from others and deal with it immediately so as not to spread to the other plants.

- It is a good idea to change the soil in potted plants every once in a while, to stop the soil from becoming stale and rotting the root system.
- Use the hand fork to till over the soil and keep it fresh.
- Having a thermometer and water meter for the plants is a good idea to ensure you are keeping your plants at their optimum comfort.
- Most flowering plants require between twelve to sixteen hours of sunlight per day.
- Plants that do not flower require between fourteen to sixteen hours of sunlight per day.
- Most plants like a lot of sunlight or a sunny room where they are not directly in the sun's path.
- Avoid moving plants from room to room or space to space. Plants get used to their position and do not like to be moved around. It can affect the plant especially if it is moved from a very sunny spot to one that is a little darker. They can go into a sort of shock.
- Some plants need a little more humidity than others so a light spray or humidifier will do the trick. Tropical plants will need a lot of humidity and may wither without it. They are usually best in or near a bathroom that gets a lot of shower steam.
- Plants need regular pruning to encourage growth, keep them neat and cut away any dead foliage that can cause problems. If leaves are left to fall off, they can turn to rot and cause soil decay which in turn can bring about all sorts of fungus, bacteria and or critters.

- Never put tea, tea bags or any form of caffeine into your planters these attract flies and all sorts of other insects that will infest the plants. The acid in these substances can also kill plants that have a low tolerance for acidity.
- Always do some research on your plant. Knowing what its classification is, longevity is, what it needs and does not need goes a long way in its care and maintenance. It also cuts down a lot of trial and error on your part.
- Not everyone has a green thumb but with a little patience, understanding and some research, you can quite easily care for and maintain healthy plants.

## Houseplant Insects

Although there are many insects that just love to make your house plants home, I will deal with the most common your plants may encounter. If you get a grip on these five culprits (which I'll mention in a moment), you're well on the way to ensure your plants have a happy home environment. But before we jump right in talking about each insect pest, let's do a something and use our power of observation.

We learned a little bit about observation earlier when we talked about inspecting your plants for general good health. That is to say, plant location, watering, light, salt buildup, etc.

We also know we got it right, when your plants look healthy and vibrant. Therefore, it is easy to notice any deterioration in the plants general appearance.

If one day you notice one or more of your plants are not looking healthy, then it's time to take a closer inspection.

Look for any leaf change that may become spotted, cupped, or distorted. Also, look at the edge or underside of leaves as well as where the leaf attaches to the stem for any indication of a silver webbing. You may also notice a substance that is sticky and shinny called honeydew on a leaf surface or underside. Although the name sounds tasty in the fruit world, it is not so for your plants because it not only indicates pest presence, it also encourages sooty mold to grow on leaves creating black or dark smudges.

Unfortunately, indoor plants don't have any natural predators to keep insects in check therefore they multiply rapidly. To reduce insect infestation, I suggest you check your plants once a week for any signs of these little critters.

## Aphid

A soft bodied insect, Aphids may come in different colors of white, green, yellow, or black. They reproduce quickly and can infest a plant in a few days. This little culprit can cause yellow and distorted leaves, leave behind a honeydew substance secreted by the insect that is usually attached on new plant growth.

## Spider Mite

For such a little critter, they can sure do a lot of damage. This insect pest is smaller than a pinhead but they can wreak havoc on your indoor plants. They feed by sucking juices from the underside of leaves causing them to turn yellow with a silver sheen and eventually the leaf will fall off. An indication of heavy spider mite infestation is webbing they leave behind and is likely the most detectible clue of their presence.

When checking your plants for spider mites, because they are so small, use a 10-power or higher magnifying glass to spot them. Another method and one I use is placing a white sheet of paper directly below a leaf and give the leaf a good shake. If there are any spider mites on the leaf they will fall off on to the paper. If you notice any tiny specks that are moving you're plant has spider mites.

These tiny pests love dusty plants, so discourage them from making your plant(s) home by frequently wiping the plant leaves with a wet cloth. You can also buy an organic product that is manufactured for use on indoor plants to control spider mites. Most garden centers or your local nursery have it available for a reasonable price.

## Mealybug

Unlike spider mites, these critters are easy to see. They are small cotton like insects that inhabit the underside of plant leaves or stems, and like the aphid they also secret a honeydew waste product.

This sticky layer will also cause a fungus called sooty mold to develop on the plants leaf. Mealybugs like most insect pests are hard to control if they get out of hand. Their feeding weakens and stunts plants causing leaf distortion and quite possibly total leaf loss.

The best way to control this pest as with others is regular plant inspection and immediate action. I inspect my plants for pests each time I water. If you notice an early presence of mealybugs, flush the area where they are located with water which will cause them to fall off. If you notice a large infestation of this pest you can rub off the colonies with a cloth.

As with any indoor plant, another option is buying an organic insecticidal soap or horticultural oils for use on your plants.

Even though these products are quite good at controlling insect pests, if you fail to check on a regular basis and your plants become completely infested, nothing will work and your only option may be to get rid of the plant. But do give it a good try before you take this drastic action.

## Whitefly

As the name says these tiny insects look like white flies and flutter around any infested plant that you happen to brush against. Like other plant pests, they feed on the underside of leaves and yes, produce honeydew. Plant growth is stunted and leaves cup up, appear dry, or turn yellow and die.

Low population of whiteflies is not usually serious and plant damage does not occur unless there is a significant increase in the population of whitefly nymphs. Unfortunately, management of heavy whitefly infestation is very difficult to control if at all with any available insecticide.

Because these critters can fly and move on to other plants, it is my advice to get rid of overly infested plant or isolate it from other plants in your home.

## Scale

As unsightly as scale may appear, they are probably the least damaging insect pest to your indoor plants.

This pest has a shell like covering for protection and is usually found on plant stems or the underside or top surface of leaves. Once they arrive they usually remain stationary having very limited movement.

Scale feeding usually produces distorted plant growth and honeydew. Small numbers are not life threatening to your plants but the honeydew they produce may cause sooty mold that greatly reduce light to the plants leaves which are used to create photosynthesis.

To rid your plants of this critter, use horticultural oils such as "Dormant oil," or "Supreme Oil," or any specialty oil for scale removal. When using any insecticide, read the directions carefully before use.

# Top 10 Indoor Tips & Tricks

Now that you understand some of the ways we can successfully grow fruits, vegetables and herbs in the comfort of our own homes, I wanted to share some tips with you that I've picked up over the years that help to summarize some of the things we have already discussed.

1. Indoor plants always tend to grow toward a light source It could be the window near the garden or the artificial grow lights. Either way, keep this in mind when setting up the garden and try to keep all plants equidistant from light sources when possible to promote vertical growth. If you notice your plants started to bend to one side or the other, consider rotating them to compensate.

2. Always make sure indoor plants receive enough light. Whether from a window, an artificial grow light or both, plants need a minimum of five hours of sunlight each day and some varieties require double that to bear fruit.

3. More plants die from improper watering than any other problem. Follow the section on watering to make sure your plants are getting exactly the right amount of water. Of course, in hydroponic and aquaponic systems,

watering is automatic but this is not the case in container gardens.

4. Don't be afraid to clean your plants from time to time. Wiping down leaves keeps dust and debris from accumulating and results in healthier, more robust plants.

5. Remember that your plants need adequate airflow to flourish. Stale, stagnant air will adversely affect plant growth. If natural airflow isn't present, use a small fan to move air over and through the garden.

6. Be mindful of temperature. Ideally, the temperature in your home should be around 70°F during the day and approximately 10° colder at night. This mimic the conditions of plants in outdoor gardens.

7. Keep records of what you have planted, when you planted it and what type of fertilizer was used. You can also monitor which plants do best near other plants. As you develop this system, you will notice trends which can be used to maximize production in future years.

8. Make sure your plants are getting enough food. Especially in container gardens, every time you water some nutrients are flushed from the soil. Either add small amounts of liquid fertilizer or add more compost

to maintain the nutrient level required for optimum growth.

9. Choose the right soil. Using soil directly from outside usually results in weeds and bacteria being introduced to the indoor growing medium. Use purpose-built potting soil or organic compost for best results.

10. Ensure your containers have proper drainage to avoid root rot and other problems usually associated with poor drainage.

# Conclusion

Thank you for making it through to the end of Houseplants for Beginners. I really hope it was informative and able to provide you with all the tools you need to achieve your goals, whatever they may be.

Houseplants liven up a home, refresh and purify the air inside your home and remove toxins. There is a houseplant to suit everyone's needs, decor and environment. Before choosing your plant(s) get a good idea of where you would like to place it/them, so you are better equipped to get the best plant for the room and space it is to fill. Remember to check on the plant's toxicity level should you have animals or children in the house.

Go window shopping for plants and get a good idea of which plants suit your needs and fit into your lifestyle. You must get a plant that you can manage and maintain to keep it and your environment a healthy one.

Choosing nice bright pots and putting the plants in areas that they will not only thrive in but are well within view will ensure that you do not forget they are there. Even if you have one or two plants to catch your eye, they will remind you that you have them and they will need some attention.

This book has also been thorough in explaining each houseplant and what they eliminate from the air. Also included was the information of what is toxic to small children and pets. Use this information to determine which plants are most likely to work in your home or office. As always, make sure that anything toxic to small children or pets is out of reach or not used in your home at all if you have either.

If you would like to use some of the houseplants in this book that are a bit harder to cultivate, visit a nursery to find the plants and get more information. The nursery where you purchase your houseplants should be able to give you more detailed care information than what is found in this book. They should also be able to help you if you run into problems after purchasing the plants.

A note on kids, if they are curious about the plants do not discourage them. In fact, the more they learn about plants and planting the better. With the green initiative in full force around the world, it is a good thing to learn about. If a kid wants to help with watering, planting and going to the nursery it is a good hobby to encourage. It is a great family bonding exercise that is both fun and educational. As long as they know that they can only tend to the plants when supervised by an adult.

Plants are not that hard to care for and with this guide, and a bit of work on your part you will be planting, growing, and maintaining instead of killing your indoor plants in no time at all.

Made in the USA
Middletown, DE
28 October 2023